D0498445

YOU CHOOSE
BOOKS

FOUNDING THE
UNITED STATES

BUILDING
A NEW NATION

An Interactive American Revolution Adventure

by Allison Lassieur

Consultant:
Richard Bell, PhD
Associate Professor of History
University of Maryland, College Park

CAPSTONE PRESS
a capstone imprint

You Choose Books are published by Capstone Press,
1710 Roe Crest Drive, North Mankato, Minnesota 56003
www.mycapstone.com

Library of Congress Cataloging-in-Publication Data
Library of Congress Cataloging-in-Publication data is available on the Library of
Congress website.

978-1-5435-1539-8 (library binding)
978-1-5435-1543-5 (paperback)

Editorial Credits
Adrian Vigliano, editor; Bobbie Nuytten, designer;
Kelly Garvin, media researcher; Kathy McColley, production specialist

Photo Credits
Alamy: Art Collection 3, 10, Classic Image, 68, Science History Images, 36; Getty
Images: Bettmann, 45, Fotosearch/Stringer, 62, FPG/Staff, 104, GraphicaArtis,
cover, Hulton Archive, 25; North Wind Picture Archive, 6, 19, 38, 49, 54, 59, 89,
94; Shutterstock/Everett Historical, 28, 72, 76, 83; Superstock/Classic Vision/age
footstock, 100

Artistic elements: Shutterstock: Abstractor, photka

Printed in Canada.
PA020

Table of Contents

ABOUT YOUR ADVENTURE

YOU feel lucky to be alive right now. For years, tension built between the colonies and Great Britain. Colonists' anger boiled over into the Revolutionary War. Against all odds, the colonists won! Now you'll be a part of creating a new nation from scratch.

In this book you'll explore how the choices people made meant the difference between life and death. The events you'll experience happened to real people.

Chapter One sets the scene. Then you choose which path to read. Follow the directions at the bottom of each page. The choices you make will change your outcome. After you finish your path, go back and read the others for new perspectives and more adventures.

YOU CHOOSE the path
you take through history.

Patriot colonists showed their support for revolution against Great Britain by tearing down reminders of the British king, such as the royal coat of arms.

CHAPTER 1

BUILDING A NATION FROM SCRATCH

It was 1781 and George Washington was in a good mood. The Revolutionary War was finally going well for his ragtag army of patriots. French allies led by Marquis de Lafayette had delivered on their promises to send guns, ships, and money. These supplies were helping Washington's army continue the fight. In Britain, support for the war was lessening. On top of that, the British army was having trouble recruiting loyalists, colonists loyal to the British crown, to their cause. The British were not defeated, but they weren't winning either.

Turn the page.

Getting here wasn't easy. The first years of the Revolution were filled with bloody defeats for Washington and the Continental army. In 1776 the British conquered New York City after five horrible battles. Washington's army was in tatters. The British seemed unstoppable. Then in 1777 the patriots scored a stunning victory at the Battle of Saratoga. This win convinced the French to support Washington's army with money and supplies. It became the turning point in the war for American freedom.

In the fall of 1781 the Battle of Yorktown changed everything. Washington commanded an army of 17,000 troops to lay siege to Yorktown, Virginia. British troops had taken over the town to rest and resupply. This gave Washington the perfect chance for an all-out attack. Two weeks later a battered British army surrendered to Washington and his army, ending the war.

Over the next two years, both sides gathered their forces and waited for a peace treaty. A few small skirmishes broke out during this time. But there would be no more large battles.

You feel lucky to be alive as big things are happening. Famous Americans seem to be everywhere. One is George Washington, the commander who won the war. There is also Benjamin Franklin and the brilliant Alexander Hamilton. American independence is being discussed in France. It is in the air on the crowded cobblestone streets of Boston and Philadelphia. A new country is rising out of war and chaos. You want to be a part of it.

To assist Benjamin Franklin during the events surrounding the signing of the Treaty of Paris, turn to page 11.

To be the son of a Massachusetts farmer during Shays' Rebellion, turn to page 39.

To serve as a clerk at the Constitutional Convention and witness the creation of the U.S. Constitution, turn to page 73.

9

Benjamin Franklin lived at the
Hôtel de Valentinois for nearly 10 years.

CHAPTER 2

THE REVOLUTION ENDS IN PARIS

You never dreamed you would work at a place as beautiful as this. The Hôtel de Valentinois, in Passy, France, is a private estate where a few people can stay for long periods of time. Valentinois belongs to your employer, Jacques-Donatien Le Ray de Chaumont. The estate is in the country, surrounded by acres of fragrant gardens and green fields. It sits on a hill overlooking the city a few miles away. You were hired as a maid a few months ago, joining an army of servants who keep the estate running.

11

Monsieur de Chaumont has allowed an American, Benjamin Franklin, to live on the estate for free. Franklin is famous all over France. He is the ambassador from the united colonies.

Turn the page.

Several universities have given him honorary degrees. Because of these honors, he likes to be called Dr. Franklin. You don't know much about the colonies or the war, but you do know that Monsieur de Chaumont supports the Americans. He has given money and supplies to their cause for independence.

Franklin has lived here for five years, since 1777. It's now January 1782. The other servants say he's charming and kind, but a bit strange. They whisper that he conducts strange experiments during lightning storms. He has a contraption called a printing press in one of his rooms.

So far, you haven't seen the elderly American ambassador who lives here. So when you're summoned to Franklin's rooms, you're surprised but excited to finally meet this American celebrity.

He greets you with a warm smile. He's quite old and bald, but he seems strong and healthy. His clothing is simple but fashionable.

"We're talking with representatives from Britain and France about a peace treaty to end the Revolutionary War in America," he begins. "I have a great deal of correspondence to which to attend. One of my secretaries has become ill. I need someone who can speak and write both French and English," he says. "You speak both languages?"

You nod, blushing. So he puts you to work. You labor until dark, translating and copying documents. Finally Franklin announces the day is done.

"You have exquisite penmanship," he says, admiring your work. "Now, if you please, make a copy of this letter, and deliver this dinner invitation."

To deliver the dinner invitation, turn to page 14.

To copy the letter, turn to page 15.

You think about how beautiful Paris is as you make your way down the cobblestone streets. You've never been to this neighborhood before. The streets are full of elegant buildings and expensive taverns. You find the address you're looking for and deliver the invitation to a stiff-looking servant who answers the door.

It would be a shame to waste a trip into Paris. But it's getting dark.

14

To hurry back to work on Dr. Franklin's letter, go to page 15.

To stop at the street market, turn to page 29.

The letter is to David Hartley, a British diplomat. It seems that Hartley wants the American ambassadors to negotiate with Britain behind France's back. Franklin will not hear of it. His letter reads: "No such Proposition as that of a separate Peace has been, is, or is ever likely to be made by me, & I believe by no authorized Person whatever in behalf of America."

"You may farther, if you please, inform his Lordship, that Mr. Adams, Mr. Laurens, Mr. Jay & myself have long since been empowered by a special Commission to treat of Peace, whenever a Negotiation shall be opened for that Purpose."

You think this over as you copy the words. It must mean that the delegates have the power to make decisions on behalf of the United States. As you continue copying the letter you see that the ambassadors plan to work with their allies to craft the new peace treaty.

Turn the page.

Every day you report to Franklin's rooms, ready to work. Dinner invitations, personal letters to friends, and requests for money make up most of the job.

On February 27 Franklin comes into the room. He is smiling. "The British government has officially voted to end the war!" he says. Now it's up to the delegates for Britain, France, and the United States of America to hammer out the details of peace.

"You have been a great help these last few weeks," he says. "If you are agreeable, I would like you to continue working for me until the peace treaty is done."

To agree to keep working for Franklin, go to page 17.

To think about it before answering, turn to page 30.

16

For the next several weeks you stay busy copying documents and organizing Franklin's correspondence. You're surprised at how active he is for such an old man! People constantly stream into the hotel for meetings with him, and he is often away on business in Paris.

One day a man arrives at the hotel, requesting a meeting with Franklin. He introduces himself as Richard Oswald, adviser to Lord Shelburne, the British prime minister. "Excellent," Franklin says. "Oswald is one of the British negotiators for peace with the United States. He's good friends with Henry Laurens, one of our delegates."

Franklin says you can stay and take notes on the meeting or return to your duties.

To stay and take notes, turn to page 18.

To return to your duties, turn to page 31.

"So Lord Shelburne has appointed you as negotiator," Franklin begins.

Mr. Oswald nods. "Your fellow peace delegate Henry Laurens can vouch for my good character as well," he says. "But I am here today because Lord Shelburne wishes to discuss promoting the happiness of mankind."

The two men launch into a discussion of peace between Britain and the colonies. You can barely keep up with everything they say! Oswald says the British sincerely want peace, and they are ready to discuss the details. Franklin says that the patriots' biggest demand is for Britain to recognize American independence.

"But," Oswald continues, "if France insists on harsh terms against Britain, we're willing to continue fighting. We have plenty of strength and resources left."

Richard Oswald (left) and Benjamin Franklin began working on a preliminary peace treaty in 1782.

"We will not do any such thing," Franklin assures him. "But I cannot speak for France at this time." He suggests that the two men meet the French ambassador another day, and Oswald agrees.

Over the next few days, letters go back and forth from Franklin to Oswald, organizing their next meeting. They agree to meet at the Palace of Versailles, the home of the French king. You're stunned when Franklin asks you to join them.

To attend the peace negotiations at Versailles, turn to page 20.

To regretfully decline, turn to page 32.

The palace is amazing. You walk through spectacular gardens, fountains, and luxurious rooms. Finally you're ushered into the meeting with Franklin's group. Soon Oswald appears, along with Charles Gravier, count de Vergennes, the French foreign minister. You furiously take notes as the three men argue and debate.

"Any peace should have a foundation of justice, and I have several demands of England," Vergennes says. He's angry because England seized several French ships against the law a few years before the war began. Clearly the British and the French don't like each other. Peace might be harder to achieve than you had thought.

"Four nations are at war against Britain," Vergennes continues. "Until they come to some agreement, we can't make any offers to Britain about peace. So we expect the first offer to come from Britain."

On the way back to Passy, Franklin says, "Oswald is a wise and honest man. I'm sure we can work out an agreement that satisfies everyone."

It's late when you get back to Passy, but the head housekeeper finds you. "A servant has no business at the royal palace!" she says. "You will return to your duties as a maid tomorrow!"

To agree to return to your maid duties, turn to page 22.

To quit, turn to page 33.

The next morning you awake to a commotion. Franklin has come to the servant's quarters! He and the head housekeeper speak privately as you wait nervously. Finally they reappear, Franklin smiling.

"Come, my dear," he says, over the irritated objections of the head housekeeper. "I'm on my way to Oswald's lodgings for more peace talks."

When you arrive the two men talk for quite some time. "The peace must be durable," Franklin says. "We don't want more war in the future." Oswald agrees heartily. Franklin asks that Britain give its Canadian colonies to the United States. Oswald won't agree to that. But he does agree that Britain should pay the colonists whose homes have been damaged or destroyed by the British.

On the way back to Passy, Franklin seems satisfied. "I believe peace is close at hand," he says. He looks kindly at you. "I'm afraid the housekeeper will not hire you back as a maid once this work is done," he says. "I would like you to stay on until the negotiations are complete. But if you would rather seek new employment, I will help you secure a good position elsewhere."

23

To see the job through with Franklin,
turn to page 24.

To find a new job, turn to page 34.

For the next several months, letters are sent among the delegation. The American delegates are Benjamin Franklin, Henry Laurens, John Adams, and John Jay. The British delegates are Richard Oswald, Lord Shelburne, and David Hartley. The group decides to negotiate a treaty without France or Spain.

The men meet constantly, hammering out the details of the treaty. The Americans have several demands. They want Britain to recognize the United States as a sovereign, independent country. All British troops must leave the colonies. They want fishing rights in the waters off Newfoundland in Britain's Canadian colonies. John Jay refuses to negotiate unless Britain recognizes the United States as a foreign nation. There is much discussion about the boundaries of the new United States.

Dear Sir, *Passy, April 14. 1782*

The Bearer having been detain'd here, I add this Line to suggest, that if the new Ministry are dispos'd to enter into a General Treaty of Peace, Mr. Laurens being set intirely at Liberty may receive such Propositions as they shall think fit to make relative to Time, Place, or any other Particulars, and come hither with them. He is acquainted that we have full Powers to treat & conclude, and that the Congress promise in our Commission to ratify and confirm, &c. —I am ever,

Yours most affectionately

B Franklin

Letters from Franklin to other delegates such as David Hartley were an important tool in treaty negotiations.

25

In early November you hand Franklin a letter. It's from John Adams. "Adams writes that we are to all meet in Paris for the final negotiations," he says. "Hopefully, we'll be signing the peace treaty."

Turn to page 26.

On November 29 the delegates meet in Paris at the Hotel d'Orleans, where John Jay is staying. You and several other secretaries frantically take notes as the group loudly discusses the final details of the treaty. Oswald argues that the Americans should pay all the debts they owe to the British. Franklin and Adams disagree, arguing that the British stole a great deal during the war. The discussion lasts for hours. Finally everyone seems to agree on the terms.

Britain will recognize the United States as a sovereign country. The boundaries of the new nation will start in the north from the Great Lakes and Britain's Canadian colonies. The southern border will be drawn on the 31st parallel. The eastern border will be at the Atlantic Ocean. The western border will be the Mississippi River. Americans will have the right to fish off the coast of Britain's Canadian colonies.

Both countries will have the right to collect debts and payments. Finally, those who have had their property taken during the war will have it returned.

The next day, November 30, both delegations accept the treaty and sign it. Franklin is overjoyed and invites the group to a celebration dinner in Passy. "It's not over yet," Franklin says. "The Continental Congress and the British Parliament must ratify the treaty."

But it's over for you. You are able to return to your job as a maid, leaving this time behind. Franklin still lives in Passy, but you rarely see him. Over the next year you rise in the ranks of servants. When a lady's maid position opens, you get it! Being a lady's maid is a well-respected job and you're grateful to have it.

In the fall of 1783, Franklin sends for you once again.

Turn the page.

Duplicate.

In the Name of the most Holy & undivided Trinity.

The Treaty of Paris clearly stated that Great Britain no longer had any claim to the United States' land or government.

"You might be pleased to know that the British and the Americans have finally ratified the treaty," he says. "I will be going to the Hotel de York in Paris for the official signing. Would you like to join my staff for the trip? You earned it with your hard work last year."

To decline, turn to page 35.

To watch the historic signing of the treaty, turn to page 36.

Fresh bread and fragrant cheese will be your supper tonight. It's past dark by the time you head for home. You're lost in thought as you walk along the side of the narrow dirt road. Somehow you don't hear the carriage barreling toward you. The driver swerves, but it's too late. Your life, so full of promise, is cut short.

THE END

To follow another path, turn to page 9.
To read the conclusion, turn to page 101.

As enjoyable as these last few weeks have been, you're not sure that being a secretary is right for you. The work is boring, and all that copying and writing make your hands and fingers cramp terribly. A maid's work isn't easy, but at least you don't have to sit at a desk all day. Franklin takes your decision with grace and thanks you again for your service. He presses a few coins into your hand in gratitude. For the rest of your life you fondly remember the famous American and his kindness.

THE END
To follow another path, turn to page 9.
To read the conclusion, turn to page 101.

The head housekeeper is not pleased that you worked for Franklin. She needs another maid but doesn't want to go through the trouble of replacing you. Reluctantly you agree to focus on your maid's duties from now on. You soon realize that you've made a terrible mistake in returning to the life of a maid. Perhaps Franklin will hire you as a permanent secretary. It won't hurt to ask.

You muster the courage to speak to Franklin. He is sympathetic but he has filled the spot and no longer needs a secretary. The housekeeper is outraged when she finds out what you did.

"You ungrateful girl," she says. "I gave you a job when no one else would. Now you think you're too good for us? Then find another place to work!" Quietly you pack your few belongings and leave, not knowing if you'll ever find a job again.

31

THE END

To follow another path, turn to page 9.
To read the conclusion, turn to page 101.

As exciting as the work sounds, you can't risk losing your permanent job here. Franklin is disappointed but he understands. "I will speak to the housekeeper," he assures you. "I will tell her what an honest, hardworking person you are. I wish you the best."

THE END

To follow another path, turn to page 9.
To read the conclusion, turn to page 101.

After everything you've experienced these last few weeks, you know there is more to life than being a maid. Franklin is sorry to see you go, but he kindly writes you a glowing letter of recommendation. Soon you've found a position as a translator and copyist in Paris. It's a life you never imagined for yourself, and you're happy.

THE END

To follow another path, turn to page 9.
To read the conclusion, turn to page 101.

It was a difficult decision, but you knew the job with Franklin would have to end sooner or later, and you would have to go back to being a maid. Franklin is true to his word. Soon you are traveling to Paris to begin a new job as a lady's maid in a French nobleman's family. You're sad to leave but excited to begin a new job in a wealthy household.

THE END

To follow another path, turn to page 9.
To read the conclusion, turn to page 101.

It was so long ago and so much has happened. You've proven your worth to the household. If you go with Franklin, you might risk losing the lady's maid job for good. As much fun as it might be to go to Paris, your duties are more important now. But you will always fondly remember your time as Franklin's secretary during such an exciting moment in history.

THE END

To follow another path, turn to page 9.
To read the conclusion, turn to page 101.

You arrive at the Hotel de York with Franklin's group on September 3, 1783. Present are the Americans Dr. Franklin, John Adams, and John Jay, and the British delegates Hartley and Oswald.

The Treaty of Paris was signed by delegates representing the United States, Great Britain, France, and Spain.

36

The British men don't look very happy, but the Americans are celebrating. Soon they all gather around a table. One by one they sign the treaty. It's hard to believe such a historic moment could be over so quickly.

Franklin asks you to do one last task. He wants you to make copies of a letter he will send to David Hartley about the signing. You carefully copy the words of this famous American:

"We sincerely rejoice with you in that event, by which the Ruler of Nations has been graciously pleased to give Peace to our two Countries."

37

You smile as you copy the rest of the letter, feeling proud to have played a small part in this moment.

THE END

To follow another path, turn to page 9.
To read the conclusion, turn to page 101.

In 1786 American workers such as blacksmiths and farmers began a series of protests against high taxes.

CHAPTER 3

THREAT OF A NEW WAR

The bloody Revolutionary War is finally over. Your father has come home to the Springfield, Massachusetts, farm where you grew up. Your family hopes to forget this terrible war and begin rebuilding.

The war has left the United States of America in terrible debt. The new government decides to raise money by levying taxes on farmers and small landowners like your father. Many cannot pay and so begin to lose their land to the government. Father explains that when the war ended, soldiers did not receive their full wages. Most men got nothing more than one month's wages.

Turn the page.

All through the spring and summer of 1786 you hear stories of farmers being arrested. Their land is taken and sold.

One morning, tax collectors show up at your farm. They demand payment. Father has nothing to give. As you watch in horror, the tax collectors haul Father to prison. He won't be released until the taxes are paid, they say. If you can't pay the taxes they will seize the farm and sell it.

You have to do something to help Father. Local farmers and citizens are organizing to protest this unfair treatment. You could go to one of the protest meetings. Or you can plead your father's case when it comes up in court in a few weeks.

To go to the protest meeting, go to page 41.

To wait and talk to the courts, turn to page 56.

40

The local tavern is packed when you arrive. One by one, people stand up and tell their stories. One man is especially angry. "I have been greatly abused, have been obliged to do more than my part in the war, and have been loaded with class taxes, town taxes, province taxes, Continental taxes, and all taxes," he shouts. "I've been pulled and hauled by sheriffs, constables, and collectors, and had my cattle sold for less than they were worth."

The room rumbles with anger. One man tries to calm everyone down. "We've sent a list of our grievances to the governor in Boston," he says. "He will listen to us."

"He ignored us!" The shouts grow louder. "The governor never replied to us, or to anyone!"

Another man stands up. "I'm Luke Day," he says. "It's time to take matters into our own hands and stop this treatment."

Turn the page.

The crowd shouts back, "We'll stop the courts from taking our land!"

The group agrees to call themselves Regulators. Their plan is to march to Northampton, Massachusetts, to shut down the town court. You leave the meeting excited to be doing something to help Father. But attacking a court of law isn't exactly what you had in mind.

To join the Regulators when they attack the courthouse, go to page 43.

To go home and think of another way, turn to page 63.

Over the next few weeks the Regulators meet and plan. Luke Day is chosen as the leader. You'll storm the Northampton Court of Common Pleas when it opens on August 29. "The Regulators aren't looking for bloodshed," Day says. "We just want our voices heard."

That morning you set out with a group toward Northampton. Other groups of Regulators fill the road toward the courthouse. Fifes and drums play merrily as you approach the town. A few war veterans wear their old uniforms and carry muskets. Everyone else, including you, is armed with clubs or swords.

A group of judges dressed in gray wigs and long black robes appear. Day stands on the courthouse steps, a petition in his hand. He tells the judges that the people refuse to pay these taxes. By now, the crowd has swelled to more than 1,500 people.

Turn the page.

The judges hastily retreat to a nearby tavern. Soon word comes back that they've agreed to close the court until November.

The Regulators whoop and holler with joy when they hear the news. As you march toward home, you approach Day and tell him your story.

"You're a brave young man," he says. "Daniel Shays and I need leaders like you to help us train a militia."

44

To help Day train the Regulators, go to page 45.

To remain part of the protesters, turn to page 48.

For the next few weeks you join Day on the West Springfield common. You help organize the men who come to join the rebellion. You feel like you're finally doing something to help Father and your family.

Turn the page.

Turn the page.

During Shays' Rebellion, protesters gathered at courthouses to try to shut them down.

After drill you take a break at the local tavern with the other men. The group begins to discuss what the Regulators will do next.

"We're not the only ones, you know," one man says. "Folks in other counties are organizing just like we are. They're electing leaders and closing down courthouses too." All agree they're lucky to have a leader like Day. He's a popular, intelligent man.

Day walks in looking angry. "The Court of Massachusetts wants to indict me, Shays, and other leaders of the Regulators," he says.

Shays is a respected Revolutionary War veteran. Like many others, he lost much of his land to government taxes. He's become the leader of the Regulators.

Shays has ordered the Regulators to march on the Springfield courthouse when it opens on September 27. That's tomorrow.

"I won't lie," Day says. "There might be bloodshed. But we're going to stop that court from meeting."

To join the Regulators at the Springfield courthouse, turn to page 51.

To return to your family, turn to page 65.

You don't have time to spend training, even if you knew how to do it. Instead you join smaller Regulator groups as they protest at courthouses around western Massachusetts. Daniel Shays, a Revolutionary War veteran, rises to become the top leader of the rebellion. He, like the other Regulators, saw his farm seized and sold by the government. You and others begin calling yourselves "Shaysites" in his honor. Many of you start wearing bits of hemlock in your hats. The hemlock represents the fight against oppression.

In town after town, Shays' protesters manage to shut down courthouses and frighten government officials. Shays gets bolder with every success. "Soon," he says, "the government will listen to the people. Soon these terrible taxes will be gone!"

In early January you hear that Governor Bowdoin has ordered Shays' arrest for treason. Shays doesn't seem bothered by this news. He's planning the biggest Regulator action yet. They will attack the federal arsenal in Springfield on January 25. The guns and weapons in the arsenal will be a big help in the fight.

Turn the page.

Disagreements among individuals sometimes led to fighting during Shays' Rebellion.

49

Men are whispering that a huge militia force will be defending the arsenal. Things are taking a deadly turn, and you don't like it. There's still time to back out. Maybe your father has advice.

To go to the arsenal with the Regulators, turn to page 60.

To visit Father in jail, turn to page 64.

When you arrive at the courthouse the next morning, the sight stuns you. Hundreds of Regulators from nearby towns crowd the square, shouting angrily. Massachusetts militia surround the courthouse, their cannons pointed directly at the crowds. Citizens watch the excitement from shop windows and doorways.

Day points to a uniformed officer. "That's Major General William Shepard. The government sent him and 800 militia here to stop us."

The judges manage to get inside the courthouse. Shays appears and joins Day. Together they order the Regulators to march around the courthouse. You join the hundreds of men shouting and chanting. The Regulators raise their clubs and swords to the sky as they march. The militia doesn't stop the Regulators. In fact, many of them join you!

Turn the page.

One militiaman catches your eye. It's Jonah, a friend of yours from the farm. He motions to you. "What are you doing with these people?" he asks. "The governor is paying us. If you need cash you should join the militia."

Before you can answer, Day finds you in the crowd. "Come on," he says. "Shays is about to speak to Shepard. He needs us behind him."

To stay with Day and the Regulators, go to page 53.

To join the Massachusetts militia, turn to page 58.

Shays rides forward and meets Major General Shepard. "On behalf of the Regulators," Shays says, "we have several demands. We ask that the court refrain from indicting anyone who has been before any previous court. We ask that the courts close until our grievances have been heard and handled. We also ask that the government disband this militia."

The major general listens respectfully. "I'm afraid I must refuse all of your demands," he says. Angry shouts ring through the air. "However," he continues, raising his hand to quiet the crowd, "the Regulators can remain here at the courthouse. You have the right to demonstrate peacefully."

"Then we will promise to leave the militia and the judges alone," Shays responds.

Turn the page.

Daniel Shays brought his experience as a Revolutionary War captain to his leadership in the Massachusetts tax protests.

The Regulators march for the rest of the day and the day after. Finally the court ends its session. The militia escorts the judges safely away and the Regulators take over the courthouse.

Shays appears, smiling. "The judges met but they didn't hand down any judgments," he says. "We won!" He addresses the crowd and tells everyone to return home. "Today is a victory," he says.

During the next few months, the Regulators spread all over western Massachusetts. They manage to shut down several courts and send the judges fleeing. But Shays is frustrated that the government isn't moving fast enough to meet the Regulators' demands. He decides to raid the Springfield Arsenal in late January. The arsenal is filled with valuable guns and weapons that the protesters need.

Turn to page 60.

Your father's case is scheduled for September 27. The family scrapes up enough money to buy necessities by selling off valuables. In the end you sell most of your belongings.

The Regulators are causing a lot of trouble. You hear of wild mobs surrounding courthouses all around western Massachusetts. You're sympathetic to their demands but can't see how their actions will help anything.

Finally September 27 arrives. The roads are filled with crowds of Regulators heading to the courthouse. Most of them carry clubs and swords, and a few have guns. They all wear sprigs of hemlock in their hats.

"What does that mean?" you ask one man.

"Unity!" he says, grinning. "The Regulators are in this together!"

The courthouse is surrounded when you arrive. Hundreds of Regulators march around the courthouse, shouting threats. A line of Massachusetts militia protect the building with guns and cannons. No one can get in or out. Your father is nowhere to be seen. It doesn't look like there will be any trials today.

You spy a familiar face in the line of militiamen. It's Jonah, a friend from home.

"What are you doing here?" you ask him.

"Protecting the country my father fought for," he replies. "These ruffians have no call to do what they're doing. Times are bad but they're traitors to the United States! You know," he continues, "we could use more men, and the Massachusetts governor is paying us."

To join the militia, turn to page 58.

To slip out of town, turn to page 66.

The lure of pay is too great. Your family needs the money. Maybe the way to help Father is to raise the money to get him out of prison. It's not the best solution but it's all you have. Reluctantly you step into the line of militia guarding the courthouse.

You and the rest of the militia stand guard for the next two days. When the court finally closes, you gratefully head for home. The militia commander, Major General Shepard, spies you with Jonah.

"Welcome, soldier," he says.

Over the next few weeks the Regulators hit several towns, closing the courthouses and intimidating the government officials. Unfortunately, they move too quickly for Shepard to muster a militia to face them. Finally, in early January, you get word from the general.

Government troops with orders to protect the
courts confronted Shays' Regulators.

The Regulators plan to attack the Springfield
Arsenal to steal guns and other weapons. The
Massachusetts militia will be there to stop them.

Turn to page 61.

Lord, it's cold, you think. It's January 25, 1787, and the four feet of snow on the ground make marching slow and difficult. You're part of Shays' army of more than a thousand Regulators on their way to the arsenal. The only thing keeping you going is the thought of Father, still in prison. You're doing this for him.

It's afternoon when the Regulator army, armed with muskets, clubs, and other weapons, arrives at the arsenal. It's surrounded by Massachusetts militia. Suddenly a cannonball whizzes over your heads. Another one follows. The men around you laugh. Shays gallops across the front of the line, shouting, "Ignore the warning shots! Keep moving!"

To stop as the rest of the army moves forward, turn to page 67.

To continue marching forward, turn to page 69.

60

You can't believe how cold it is. It's been snowing heavily all night. Now it's dawn and you're waiting for Shays' Regulators to show up. The militia, more than 1,200 strong, is ready. The soldiers are armed with muskets, cannons, and howitzer guns. Howitzers fire grapeshot, deadly lead balls that can rip through a man's body in an instant. Major General Shepard rides up and down the line, offering encouragement. Despite the cold, excitement ripples through the lines.

It's well after noon when the shout finally comes. "There they are!" A line of Regulators appears, marching slowly through the deep snow.

"Fire warning shots!" Shepard orders.

BOOM! BOOM! Cannonballs soar above the Regulators' heads. You expect them to stop, or at least slow down. But they keep moving forward!

Turn the page.

Shays' army expected little resistance from the men guarding the Springfield Arsenal, but they were surprised.

62

They don't seem to realize the danger they face. You almost can't watch as Shepard orders the artillery to fire directly into the approaching group of men.

To move behind the guns for safety,
turn to page 70.

To stand your ground, turn to page 71.

You and your family sell nearly every possession you own. You ask relatives for anything they can give, which isn't much. It isn't enough to pay the heavy taxes and release Father from jail. The collectors come and take the farm, then set Father free. He is worn and tired from the ordeal. Your family packs its few remaining belongings and sets out for Boston, leaving its old life behind.

THE END

To follow another path, turn to page 9.
To read the conclusion, turn to page 101.

Father is thin and worn but still defiant. "I fought for this country to be free," he says. "I helped make this new nation. But I won't let my son throw away his life with a bunch of ruffians! I don't care how noble they think they are." He urges you to continue protesting and fighting, but not to get involved in an actual battle.

Your decision is made. You'll sit out the attack on the arsenal. You take your belongings and return to your family.

64

THE END
To follow another path, turn to page 9.
To read the conclusion, turn to page 101.

That night you tell your mother what is to happen the next day. Her worried look breaks your heart. "Don't do this," she pleads. "Your father is already in jail. I don't want you to join him or—worse—get killed. It's too dangerous."

You toss and turn all night, thinking it over. When dawn finally comes you've made your decision. Protesting unfair taxes isn't worth sacrificing your life. You stay home, hoping Day and the other Regulators won't think badly of you.

THE END

To follow another path, turn to page 9.
To read the conclusion, turn to page 101.

The money isn't worth standing against the protesters. They curse and shout at you. Fear makes you forget why you're there in the first place. All you can think about is getting home in one piece. A group of militia blocks the road. "Halt!" the men shout, pointing their muskets at you.

"I'm not one of them!" you say, raising your hands.

"That's for the judge to work out," one soldier says, nudging you in the ribs. "Come with me." The next thing you know you're sitting in a damp jail cell, listening to the shouts of the mob nearby. You have no idea how long you'll be stuck here before you stand before a judge. All you know is that you're not getting out of here anytime soon.

THE END

To follow another path, turn to page 9.
To read the conclusion, turn to page 101.

Those cannonballs looked a little too close for your liking. You drop out of line as the rest of the army marches on. Just as you're starting to feel embarrassed by your cowardice, a thunderous *BOOM* shakes the ground. Cannonballs crash into the Regulators, scattering the men as they scream in pain.

Gunfire from a howitzer is next. You watch as the howitzer fires canisters full of deadly grapeshot. These small lead balls do terrible damage. The white snow is stained red as bodies fall everywhere. The Regulators run to the rear, almost trampling you as they flee.

Shays is nowhere to be seen. Everyone is confused. No one seems to know what to do. Another round of cannon fire makes the decision for you. Turning, you run as fast as you can. Other Regulators shout "Murderers!" as they retreat.

Turn the page.

Four of Shays' rebels were killed in the attack on the Springfield Arsenal.

You spot Shays on his horse, shouting orders. But it's no use. You don't stop until you get home. As you breathlessly describe the battle, one thing becomes clear. Shays' Rebellion is over.

THE END

To follow another path, turn to page 9.
To read the conclusion, turn to page 101.

You hope the militia won't shoot to kill. After all, the Regulators are tired, cold, and have only clubs and muskets. They are no match for the militia's deadly artillery. Still, the Regulator army moves forward, determined to capture the arsenal.

Suddenly a tremendous *BOOM* fills the air as cannonballs blast into the Regulators. Some men scream and run as others fall, their blood staining the white snow red. Someone yells "Retreat!" and that's the last word you hear. You fall softly into the deep snow, your own blood mingling with the blood of the other dead and wounded.

69

THE END

To follow another path, turn to page 9.
To read the conclusion, turn to page 101.

Men are loading the heavy howitzer gun as you move to the back. They are clumsy and something goes wrong. Suddenly a deafening roar comes from the howitzer and you're blown off your feet. In a flash you rise into the air, fly backward, and land softly in a snowbank. Your friend Jonah runs to you, followed by other soldiers. They all have horrified looks on their faces. You don't feel any pain at all, but you can't seem to get up out of the snow.

"Stay still, friend," Jonah says, tears streaming down his face. "You're going to be fine." The snow around you has turned bright red. You're confused as to how all that blood got there. Then suddenly you feel tired. You squeeze Jonah's hand and close your eyes for good.

THE END

To follow another path, turn to page 9.
To read the conclusion, turn to page 101.

You've never been this scared in your life, but you don't move. The artillery blasts straight into the oncoming men. Blood and screams fill the air as the first rounds hit. Bodies fall into the red-stained snow. The rest of the Regulators pause, then they all turn and flee, leaving their dead and wounded behind.

The soldiers tend to the dead and wounded Regulators. Shepard regroups his forces to chase what's left of Shays' army. On February 4, 1787, Shepard's army joins another militia force commanded by General Benjamin Lincoln. Together the militias surprise Shays' army and soundly defeat the Regulators. Shays escapes to New Hampshire along with a few hundred men, but Shays' Rebellion is over.

THE END

To follow another path, turn to page 9.
To read the conclusion, turn to page 101.

ARTICLES

OF

CONFEDERATION

AND

PERPETUAL UNION

BETWEEN THE

STATES

OF

NEW-HAMPSHIRE, MASSACHUSETTS-BAY, RHODE-ISLAND
AND PROVIDENCE PLANTATIONS, CONNECTICUT, NEW-
YORK, NEW-JERSEY, PENNSYLVANIA, DELAWARE, MARY-
LAND, VIRGINIA, NORTH-CAROLINA, SOUTH-CAROLINA
AND GEORGIA.

*The Articles of Confederation served as
the first constitution of the United States.*

LANCASTER, (PENNSYLVANIA,) PRINTED:

BOSTON, RE-PRINTED BY JOHN GILL,
PRINTER TO THE GENERAL ASSEMBLY.
M,DCC,LXXVII.

CHAPTER 4

CREATING THE CONSTITUTION

After the Revolutionary War, the Articles of Confederation are the law of the land. The Continental Congress has very little power. Instead, the laws allow each state to form its own government. Each state can make its own money, raise armies, control trade, and collect taxes. This causes confusion and anger everywhere.

People have begun to realize the new country needs a new system. A strong, centralized government could bring the states together under one set of laws for all Americans.

None of this affects you much. For the last few years you've been an apprentice clerk at a successful store in downtown Philadelphia.

73

Turn the page.

It's your job to keep track of all the paperwork, to write letters, and to collect payments from customers. In the spring of 1787, you hear some exciting news. There's going to be a convention in your hometown of Philadelphia to revise the Articles of Confederation. Every state has chosen delegates for the meeting.

A few weeks later James Madison, a delegate to the convention, arrives from Virginia. He is staying at Mrs. House's boardinghouse. Surely the delegates will need assistants, you think. You've become a little bored with the life of a store clerk and you're ready for a challenge.

One morning you present yourself at Mrs. House's establishment. Madison is there, along with a distinguished-looking man. After a few moments you feel shocked as you recognize him. How could you not have known the famous George Washington?

When he arrived in Philadelphia, he rode over the Schuylkill River on a floating bridge. Troops fired a 13-gun salute in his honor. You joined a cheering crowd lined up along the street to watch him pass.

You take a deep breath and introduce yourself. "I'm intelligent, I'm a hard worker, and I have excellent penmanship," you explain. "I can take notes quickly and clearly. I would be a good secretary for any of the delegates."

Madison smiles. "That's the spirit we need in our new country, wouldn't you say, George?"

Washington nods. "You will go far in life, young man," he says. "I'm George Washington, delegate from Virginia." You nod, speechless. "I may have need of an assistant during the meetings."

Turn the page.

After leading colonial forces to victory over the British in the Revolutionary War, George Washington became a national hero.

"Yes," Washington continues, nodding, "Having a clerk could be useful."

"I, too, am in need of an assistant during the convention," Madison says.

To work as Washington's clerk, go to page 77.

To assist Madison during the convention, turn to page 84.

How can you possibly refuse America's greatest hero? As the commander of the Continental army, he won the Revolutionary War for America.

"I thought you'd retired after the war," you blurt, instantly embarrassed.

"I thought I had," Washington says, half smiling. "But James here talked me into becoming a delegate for the convention." Washington rises. "Come, walk with me, I wish to pay my respects to Dr. Franklin."

Of course he's talking about Benjamin Franklin, the most famous man in Philadelphia. You bid Madison goodbye and follow Washington onto the street.

Turn the page.

Instantly everyone recognizes the tall, elegantly dressed Washington. He doesn't get half a block before a crowd of well-wishers encircles him.

"Does this happen often?" you ask as you're jostled to and fro.

"Yes, but I don't mind," Washington replies as the people press forward. "I may be here a while. If you don't wish to wait, meet me at the Pennsylvania State House on the first day of the convention."

To stay with Washington, go to page 79.

To join him on the first day of the convention, turn to page 82.

It's marvelous to watch Washington politely shake hands and smile as he gently pushes through the crowd. Finally you make it to Franklin's house. The pleasant square brick home sits far back from the street.

You've never met Franklin but you've heard about him all your life. When he returned from France in 1785 the whole city turned out to see him. There were parades, flags waving from every house, cannons booming in welcome, and church bells ringing through the streets. You follow a servant through the house to the back garden where Franklin sits beneath a large tree. He is old and rather fat, with short, white hair and a bald spot on the middle of his head.

Turn the page.

"George, so good to see you!" Franklin exclaims, taking Washington by the hands. "And who is this young man?" You barely get your name out, you're so nervous. Fortunately, Franklin doesn't notice.

The two men talk for hours. You try to follow their conversation even when you don't understand what they are discussing. As dinnertime approaches, Washington turns to you.

"Thank you for attending me," he says kindly. "I'm sure you want to leave us old men to our chatter. I will see you when the convention starts on May 25."

To go home, turn to page 81.

To go to a tavern, turn to page 92.

Your family can't believe your good fortune. Father is beside himself with pride. "Think of the career you'll have, my son!" he says. Mother beams. Your brothers and sisters are jealous that you have met the great Franklin and Washington in the same day! As you climb into bed, the reality of what happened today hits you. You don't know what is about to happen. You just hope you're worthy to take part in it.

81

Turn to page 82.

It's a miserable, rainy May morning when you set out for the State House. The State House is famous for being the place where the Declaration of Independence was signed in 1776.

There's a commotion on the street, and you turn to see Benjamin Franklin approaching. He's seated in a glass-windowed sedan chair, carried by four men. Franklin waves as delegates gaze at the sight. Only Franklin could make an entrance like this.

Inside it's hot and muggy. The first order of business is to elect a president of the convention. Washington is the unanimous choice. At first he says no. "I'm not a politician," he says. "I'm not here to gain power." But the other delegates urge him to accept, so he finally does. He takes his place at the front, in a large chair painted with a rising sun.

Washington's leadership at the Constitutional Convention impressed his fellow delegates.

The heat makes you dizzy and light-headed. You're not sure how you'll make it through the next few weeks. Washington leans toward you. "You're free to go," he says kindly, seeing your distress.

To leave the convention, turn to page 93.

To stay, turn to page 94.

Your job is to take notes and help Madison with his errands. You agree to meet him outside the State House steps on the first day of the convention, May 25. Excitement is running high, both inside the State House and outside. Everyone in Philadelphia knows about the Constitutional Convention. One newspaper wrote, "Upon the event of this great council depends everything that can be essential to the dignity and stability of the national character."

The delegates elect Washington as president and vote on a few rules. The first to which they all agree is that the deliberations will be kept secret. Then Edmund Randolph from Virginia steps forward. He presents a radical plan called the Virginia Plan, to form an entirely new government. After much debate, the convention votes in favor of one of the proposals in the Virginia Plan.

The proposal creates three branches of government: an executive, legislature, and judiciary. The proposal also explains that the legislature should consist of two chambers.

But no one can agree on how the people will be represented. Some delegates want representation based on population. Others insist that each state should have only one vote, no matter how many people live there.

To listen to the argument for one state, one vote, turn to page 86.

To listen to the argument of votes based on population, turn to page 87.

"We must allow all states to have the same voting power!" That is the argument from the delegates representing small states such as Delaware and New Jersey. New Jersey delegate William Paterson says giving more power to larger, more populated states is like giving more votes to the rich.

Delegates from less populated, slave-owning states such as Georgia agree. They want as much power in Congress as the larger states would have. Paterson threatens to withdraw from the convention over this. You think Paterson's argument is solid. But will the rest of the delegates agree?

To hear the opposing argument, go to page 87.

To see the delegates' final agreement, turn to page 88.

James Wilson from Pennsylvania also strongly believes that each state should be equal in Congress. But he thinks that the way to have equality is to have each state represented based on the size of its population. He argues that it is a matter of simple democracy. "An equal number of people should have an equal number of representatives. Shall New Jersey have the same right or influence in the councils of the nation with Pennsylvania? I say no. It is unjust!"

The delegates from smaller, less populated states grow angry. They support the idea that each state should have the same number of representatives regardless of population. They urge the delegates to vote against Wilson.

The larger states side with Wilson, but he doesn't have enough votes to win the argument. What can he do to convince the delegates?

To see how the delegates finally vote, turn to page 88.

The delegates are so angry about this issue that they refuse to discuss it for several days. During that time James Wilson of Pennsylvania comes up with a way to get the smaller, slave-owning states on his side. On June 11 he offers a new proposal. Representation in Congress will be based on the population of free people, plus three-fifths of all others.

Counting one enslaved person as three-fifths of a person boosts the slave-owning states' population numbers. This gives them more power. Of course delegates from slave-owning states quickly agree to this compromise. The delegates from Connecticut then propose that the states each have an equal vote. After several more weeks of furious debate, the proposals pass—by one vote! One house of Congress will be the House of Representatives, with members determined by state population. The other house will be called the Senate. There, all states receive equal representation.

Constitutional Convention delegates discussed each section of the Constitution in great detail.

You're exhausted and disappointed in the delegates over their compromise on slavery. Your family has been against it for a long time. It's hard to listen to the delegates speak of human beings as property. It's especially difficult because Madison is a slave owner. You don't know if you can work with him any longer.

To stay as Madison's clerk until the end, turn to page 90.

To leave the convention over slavery, turn to page 97.

89

After much thought you decide that you'll stay to bear witness to this great event. Unfortunately, the debate over representation nearly tears the convention apart. You're glad when it's finally over.

The hot summer stretches on. The delegates meet each day to come up with rules for a new government. For instance, the delegates make rules that allow the federal government to create currency, regulate the economy, and raise an army for the defense of the nation. They decide that the nation's president will serve a four-year term. They also give the president broad powers to deal with foreign governments.

Finally on September 17 the convention gathers to sign the Constitution. As the delegates sign the document, you read the beginning.

"We the people of the United States, in Order to form a more perfect Union . . . do ordain and establish this Constitution for the United States of America."

Madison shakes your hand and thanks you for your service. "The delegates are gathering for a farewell dinner," he says. "You are cordially invited."

To decline the invitation, turn to page 98.

To join Madison and the delegates, turn to page 99.

Your friends won't believe what's happened to you! You find them in the City Tavern and tell them about your adventures. Many hours later, you head for home. It's late and you don't see the carriage that is racing down the cobblestone streets. You jump out of the way, but it's too late. You slowly make your way home on an injured leg. The next morning you wake up in terrible pain. Your weeping family surrounds you.

"Your leg is broken in several places," the doctor says grimly. "It will be months before you can walk again." The convention is long over by the time you heal. You wish you could have been there to experience the rest of it.

92

THE END

To follow another path, turn to page 9.
To read the conclusion, turn to page 101.

It wasn't the heat that made you feel strange. Once you're home, Mother declares you have a fever. For several days you lie in bed, sick. You hear that the convention is closed and the deliberations secret. When you recover, you join the groups of curious people who linger outside the State House. Everyone is hoping for a glimpse of one of the famous figures inside. You never see Washington or Madison again, but you will always recall their kindness.

THE END

To follow another path, turn to page 9.
To read the conclusion, turn to page 101.

Not even sickness will make you leave Washington's side. Washington, wearing his old military uniform, doesn't say much as the delegates debate and discuss different ideas. "I'm here to maintain order if the delegates get overly rowdy," he says.

By early September 1787, the Constitutional Convention had settled on a draft of the Constitution and begun work to polish it into a finished document.

The convention drags on through the broiling hot summer. You take notes during the day and accompany Washington and the delegates to dinner some evenings. Over time you become familiar with many of the delegates. There is Franklin, always witty and charming. James Madison is constantly arguing for a brand new government. War hero Alexander Hamilton is brilliant but talks a lot. George Mason from Virginia is deeply opposed to slavery and supports the rights of all. Connecticut delegate Roger Sherman supports fairness and compromise in all the deliberations.

By September the convention has finished a draft of the new Constitution. On September 17, 1787, 38 of 41 delegates present sign the new Constitution. The Constitution will now become law if it is ratified by 9 of the 13 new states.

Turn the page.

When the signing is done, Washington shakes your hand. "We've made history here," he says. "I'm happy that you were a part of it. Thank you for your service to the new United States government."

THE END

To follow another path, turn to page 9.
To read the conclusion, turn to page 101.

You struggle to decide what to tell Madison. He is one of the most powerful, famous men in America. You're just a 14-year-old apprentice. But Madison is also a slave owner. If you told him you're leaving because you're against the idea of people owning other people he might be angry. He could use his influence to keep anyone else from hiring you in the future. In the end you simply explain that you must get back to your apprenticeship. He seems to understand and wishes you well. You regret leaving this historic convention, but you're happy that you were able to be a part of it.

97

THE END

To follow another path, turn to page 9.
To read the conclusion, turn to page 101.

It sounds like fun, but you promised your family you'd be home for dinner. As you turn to leave, you see Franklin. This might be your last chance to speak to him. When you approach, he points to the chair Washington has been sitting in for the last four months.

"Have you noticed the back of the chair?" he says aloud to the few people near him. He points to the painted sun on the back. "Often during the course of these deliberations, with my hopes and fears, I've found it difficult to know if this is the rising or the setting sun. But now, I have the happiness to know it is the rising, not the setting, sun."

It is a new beginning for our brand new country, you think, as you step out of the State House for the last time.

THE END

To follow another path, turn to page 9.
To read the conclusion, turn to page 101.

98

The City Tavern is crowded and loud. Washington, Madison, and most of the other delegates are eating and drinking happily. Musicians play lively tunes. The food is delicious. You spend the rest of the evening enjoying yourself. When it's time to leave, Washington bids you farewell. Madison shakes your hand and thanks you again for your service. For the rest of your life you'll remember how you were witness to history.

THE END

To follow another path, turn to page 9.
To read the conclusion, turn to page 101.

The surrender of British forces at Yorktown was an important moment in the founding of the United States.

CHAPTER 5

PROMISE OF FREEDOM

The British surrender at Yorktown in 1781 brought relief and excitement to the patriot fighters. Benjamin Franklin had been the ambassador to France since 1776. After negotiating the Treaty of Paris, he remained in Passy until 1785, when Thomas Jefferson replaced him as the French ambassador. The Treaty of Paris marked the end of the terrible war. The newly free Americans looked forward to peace and prosperity. They got neither.

For a time, things seemed to be improving. But the new country faced crushing debt. The solution seemed to be raising taxes. Daniel Shays and his rebellion put a stop to that idea.

Shays survived the bloody battle at the Springfield Arsenal. He was a wanted man for his role in the rebellion. He spent several years on the run from the law. Finally, in 1788, Shays was pardoned by the state of Massachusetts.

The rebellion forced the country to rethink the Articles of Confederation. The United States needed a new, stronger government. The delegates who gathered in Philadelphia in 1787 for the Constitutional Convention understood the seriousness of their task. The future of the country for which they had fought and killed was at stake. Over a blistering hot summer, they talked and debated until they created a framework for a new kind of government. The result was a remarkable document.

After the Constitutional Convention, each state had to ratify the new Constitution. Nine of the 13 states had to ratify the Constitution before it could become law. The delegates went back to their states and organized support. For months, state legislators debated whether to accept the Constitution. Many people were against it. Some wanted to go back to the Articles of Confederation. Others argued that the Constitution didn't go far enough. They wanted to add a Bill of Rights to the document.

Three delegates came up with a plan to whip up support for the Constitution. Alexander Hamilton and John Jay of New York, and James Madison of Virginia decided to write a series of essays. The essays, called the "Federalist Papers," would explain how great the Constitution was. On June 21, 1788, New Hampshire became the ninth state to ratify the Constitution, joining Delaware, Pennsylvania, New Jersey, Georgia, Connecticut, Massachusetts, Maryland, and South Carolina.

President Washington's (right) first cabinet included Henry Knox (seated, left), Thomas Jefferson (standing, left), Edmund Randolph (center), and Alexander Hamilton (second to right).

Now it was time to put the Constitution to work. The new Congress unanimously elected George Washington as the first president of the United States on February 4, 1789. He didn't want to be president. But he believed it was his duty to accept, so he did. Washington chose Thomas Jefferson as his secretary of state. Alexander Hamilton became the first Treasury secretary.

Benjamin Franklin lived to see his friend Washington become president. Franklin died in 1790. After eight years in office, Washington went back to his home in Mount Vernon, Virginia, in 1797. Two years later Washington died at home. Alexander Hamilton used his time as Treasury secretary to develop the U.S. economic system. He was shot and killed in 1804 in a duel with Vice President Aaron Burr. In 1801 Thomas Jefferson became the third President of the United States, and James Madison became the fourth in 1809. John Jay served as the first Chief Justice of the United States Supreme Court and second governor of New York.

All of these people played a part in creating the U.S. Constitution and our country. They knew they were building a government from scratch. But they didn't know they were creating something else—a country that would become a symbol of freedom and independence to the world.

TIMELINE

April 1775—The fighting begins in the American Revolution in the Battles of Lexington and Concord

May 10, 1775—The Second Continental Congress meets in Philadelphia

July 4, 1776—The colonies officially sign the Declaration of Independence, asserting their independence from Britain

November 15, 1777—The Continental Congress adopts the Articles of Confederation

February 6, 1778—The Treaties of Alliance and of Amity and Commerce are signed with the French

March 1, 1781—The Articles of Confederation are fully ratified by all thirteen states

September 3, 1783—The Treaty of Paris officially ends the American Revolution; Great Britain recognizes the independence of the United States of America

1786—Shays' Rebellion begins in western Massachusetts

1787—Shays' Rebellion is defeated

1787—The Constitutional Convention creates the United States Constitution

September 17, 1787—The Constitution is signed by 38 of the 41 delegates to the Constitutional Convention

1788—A majority of states ratify the Constitution

March 4, 1789—George Washington begins serving as first president of the United States

OTHER PATHS TO EXPLORE

In this book, you've seen how events from the past look different from three points of view. Perspectives on history are as varied as the people who lived it. Seeing history from many points of view is an important part of understanding it. Here are ideas for other early American points of view to explore.

+ Daniel Shays and the Regulators protested what they considered to be unfair taxes by shutting down the courts. The Massachusetts militia ultimately defeated them in January 1787. If Shays and the Regulators had won that day, what might have happened next?

+ At the Constitutional Convention, James Wilson came up with what is called the Three-Fifths Compromise. An enslaved black person would be counted as three-fifths of a white person. Why would antislavery delegates go along with this compromise? How did this compromise change the balance of power among the states?

READ MORE

Jacobson, Bray. *The US Constitution*. A Look at U.S. History. New York: Gareth Stevens Publishing, 2017.

Krull, Kathleen. *A Kid's Guide to the American Revolution*. New York: HarperCollins, 2018.

Manger, Katherine. *The U.S. Constitution*. Let's Find Out! Primary Sources. New York: Britannica Educational Publishing, 2017.

Roxburgh, Ellis. *Shays' Rebellion*. Rebellions, Revolts, and Uprisings. New York: Gareth Stevens Publishing, 2017.

INTERNET SITES

Use FactHound to find Internet sites related to this book.

Visit *www.facthound.com*

Just type in 9781543515398 and go.

GLOSSARY

ambassador (am-BA-suh-duhr)—government official who represents his or her country in a foreign country

apprentice (uh-PREN-tiss)—someone who learns a trade by working with a skilled person

compromise (KAHM-pruh-myz)—settlement in which each side gives up part of its demands and agrees to the final product

delegate (DEL-uh-guht)—a person who represents a larger group of people at a meeting

grievance (GREE-vuhns)—formal expression of a complaint against an unjust or unfair act

howitzer (HOU-uht-sur)—a cannon that shoots explosive shells long distances

indict (in-DIYT)—to charge with a crime

militia (muh-LISH-uh)—group of volunteer citizens organized to fight, but who are not professional soldiers

negotiation (ni-GOH-shee-ay-shun)—talking to reach an agreement

ratify (RAT-uh-fie)—formally approve

sovereign (SAHV-uh-rehn)—having an independent government

BIBLIOGRAPHY

Carp, Benjamin. *Defiance of the Patriots.* New Haven, Conn.: Yale University Press, 2010.

Ellis, Joseph J. *American Creation: Triumphs and Tragedies at the Founding of the Republic.* New York: Knopf, 2007.

Franklin, Benjamin. *The Life of Benjamin Franklin, Written By Himself.* New York: Cambridge University Press, 2011.

Richards, Leonard. *Shays's Rebellion: The American Revolution's Final Battle.* Philadelphia: University of Pennsylvania Press, 2002.

Stewart, David O. *The Summer of 1787: The Men Who Invented the Constitution.* New York: Simon & Schuster, 2007.

Wood, Gordon S. *The American Revolution: A History.* New York: Modern Library, 2002.

INDEX